ANTEDILUVIAN

PITT POETRY SERIES
NANCY KRYGOWSKI
AND JEFFREY MCDANIEL,
EDITORS

ANTEDILUVIAN

KAMERYN ALEXA CARTER

UNIVERSITY OF
PITTSBURGH PRESS

Published by the University of Pittsburgh Press, Pittsburgh, Pa., 15260

Manufactured in the United States of America
Printed on acid-free paper
10 9 8 7 6 5 4 3 2 1

ISBN 13: 978-0-8229-6767-5
ISBN 10: 0-8229-6767-7

Cover art: Na Chainkua Reindorf, *Peli: You don't play games with danger*, 2020. Gouche on watercolor paper, 44 x 62 in. Image courtesy of Anthony Brunelli Fine Arts. © Na Chainkua Reindorf
Cover design: Melissa Dias-Mandoly

Publisher: University of Pittsburgh Press, 7500 Thomas Blvd., 4th floor, Pittsburgh, PA 15260, United States, www.upittpress.org

EU Authorized Representative: Easy Access System Europe, Mustamäe tee 50, 10621 Tallinn, Estonia, gpsr.requests@easproject.com

CONTENTS

ANTEDILUVIAN

St. John the Baptist Bearing Witness

The dog enters with a slaughtered rabbit in his mouth like a twisted pietà. At high noon every clock in the house sucks its teeth. I wanted to be shown something transcendent, so I take what I am given—the dog's bloody offering at my feet. My mood disorder is impervious to metaphor. Slips away from simile. It isn't like or as, isn't is. The manic mystic is a myth. Still, I am before you today to extend the invitation—synapse rupture, syntax snap. Won't you come? I cannot say what god is waiting, only that when they call me, I come barreling. Only that the weight of wandering has led me back from the wilderness to bear witness to what I have seen—the rabbit: limp ligament of gore and glory, glinting sun-electric—only that when they call me, I come.

Outside

Yes, I lost the lottery. I can never write about the moon again, only the neon ball locked between the dog's fangs, only what it's like to see without glasses. I buy expensive oils which come in dark bottles labeled *Sleep*. I buy expensive oils which come doorstep so I need not leave. The eggplant talks to me. The dog talks to me but I don't know Basque. The weeks wind so tight. Drowning was long ago but it's come up again, vomiting lake onto the butcher block in the kitchen. Depression commercial crudités. This lottery is not a game. One cannot describe the taste of fennel as it is unlike anything else. Hold, I have just been informed of black liquorice. Outside the poem the phone is ringing. Pick it up.

Still Life

Outside, I might have had teeth. I might have been an antelope or the lion which devours it. I might have been an infant, latching. Inside I am a creature in a silk blouse: cockscomb mane on edge, gaping my empty mouth like a bloody, hollowed pomegranate. I wake beclouded by bloodlust—anachronism antedomestic. So often I wake clutching my arms. Inside is wicked, elastic—everything a trick of the intellect, of the iris. When I can grin and bear it, I behold my own grotesque face in the mirror. *Are you there?* The antelope bids.

Commodity Fetish

They put me under
the wire and danger
comes like water
from a comet. I am
sprinting at the top
of my lungs. Soon
my teeth will be sold
in an online shop
called Whatsoever
ThingsAreLovely—
nestled inside
the velvet mouth
of a faux Fabergé egg.

I checked YES at intake.
I answered the questions
earnestly. I wrote, "It is
not natural to hold anything
at the neck." Even a shot
spruce grouse writhing
in the dirt.

The interviewer asks
how it feels to know
I will soon die
of consumption.

I am sprinting
for my life.

Discharge

In the Free World, I'm allowed pens
but it's lonely among the living—
cetacean strandings galore
so many stenographers
choking to death on date-pits

So many beached bodies
in repose

This morning, I sliced my index
cutting quince with a dull knife
and bled nasturtium all over
the counter

In the Free World: back
to silk scarves. Back
to knives. Back to cable.
Back to bathtub. Back
to you, with the weather.
Back to world. Back
to free. Back to shoes. Back
to Jewel-Osco. Back
to orange pith in nail bed.

Back to ledges everywhere,
ripe for the leaping

Two Wings to Veil My Face

I say *Jesus wept* in place
of weeping. I say, *I was*
born submerged. Proposition:
wilted salad in a plastic bag.
Corollary: ain't'a that good news?

Today I farewelled my dead
in the drive-thru funeral parlor—
velvet curtains parting
for the dearly departed
with the engine still awake.
I can only describe myself
as capsized. Somewhere a stone
is rolled away on a good Friday,
but not here. Somewhere a stone
fruit gives under the weight
of a hungry thumb.

He wept.

A Party at Annie's

I spend the evening averting my eyes,
chasing after an evasive vibration
by the makeshift bar and reciting incantations
that only I could surmise
were Berryman—lines disarrayed and revised.
Awaiting Loïe with impatience,
the *Collected* beneath my arm like a hymnal.

And when the tide of my mood comes roaring,
I will search the room for Loïe's absinthe eyes and steal
us away into the street on my heels
in search of a store that still sells loosies. It's pouring.
But I will search for that adoring
gaze and steel
myself against the rain.

Interior

Proposition

Once, you moved freely through the cobweb between realms. Now you are double-latched, endangered leafwing: locked door, locked mind.

Proof

In the case of solitude (a condition of inside) self-recognition remains a tenuous tendon.

Corollary 1

You create a taxonomy of all the clandestine betrayals of the mind: marginalia on the back of a yellowed receipt. You arrange pitted dates in a line on your kitchen table.

Corollary 2

Manon slips in and out of diegetic, in and out and in, Leontyne's timbre slicing through stale air.

Counterargument

Recognition of self requires only consciousness. Consciousness is one proof for alive.

Scholium

What do you feel?

Proposition

Inside, motion is an illusion.

Proof

The presence of motion requires time elapsing, just as it requires stasis by contrast. The Fletcher's Paradox, timid toxophilite.

Corollary 1

Inside is purgatory, linear time: a logical absurdity.

Corollary 2

Motion requires impetus. Gravity. Body. Will. The body's animation requires synchronous communication between the brain and other parts of the body.

Corollary 3

I remain inside because my brain falsely simulates danger,
rupturing synchronous communication
between the brain and other parts of the body.
I remain inside because I feel little to no impetus. I remain inside
because I have no body.
I remain inside because I am inanimate. I remain inside because I
cannot get out.

Corollary 4

Agora: public open assembly gathering

Corollary 5

Motion is displacement. Transportation from one location to another, however minute, even if the arm falls back to one's side after being raised to swipe away the fallen eyelash. Even if breath. Inside is a nowhereplace.

Corollary 6

If motion is an illusion, the absence of motion is a temporal suspension.

Corollary 7

I cannot trust my senses. I cannot know what images, what sensations are sleights of mind. Because I am ruptured, I must assume everything has the potential to be illusory.

Counterargument

I rode a bicycle in figure eights at the street's dead end. My ponytails were pendulums.

Countercounterargument

I must remember that time is nonlinear, and inside is atemporal. Therefore I am always, and never, and not yet.

Counterproof

I am inside and despite my searching, I cannot find where motion was once written in muscle. This is to say, who is to say it could be. The laws of inside negate outside. I cannot remember. I cannot let myself be tantalized by the possibility of air air air

Proposition

The condition of inside is infinite.

Scholium

How long has it been?

Counterargument

Inside is a condition. Condition meaning contingent factor. Condition meaning illness. Condition meaning if. Condition(s) meaning environment. Condition meaning conditional. Meaning so long as. Condition meaning state of being. State of being meaning fungible. Malleable. Changeable. Fecund. Matter. Ephemera. Meaning temporary. Meaning time. Meaning the possibility of motion. Meaning possible. Meaning possible

Devil-May-Care

I'm a fabulist in a spangled cloak.
I'm a theist on the run— ink blurred
by a dragged sleeve. I'm sitting
in an ill-fitting dermis. I am
a mycologist: minor arcana
of chanterelles scattered
before me—their bowing folds—
a different divination.

Such wonders—fated, furled,
fettered, furied. If you must
know, I'm a pantheon adorned
in fugue— recapitulation,
rememory.

When I was dead, I was unknowing
of my nakedness. I had a tonic
clonic to restore me. Every new day,
a birthday fête. Forgive my cavalierness.
We don't mean it. I cannot contain
my spirit. Neither multitudes, in fact.
I cannot contain myself, orotund
ornament— such interminable wonder.

Theoria

The path to me is via negativa—
apophatic, apoplectic, here is what
I isn't: a theophany burning rum baba
black. It's good to see you—a little
more psychotherapy and the clockarms
may simply halt. Insist, and I can tell you
what I am. I'm a practical mystic:
approachable at the grocery or in line
at the movies. A little more cognitive
and I'll behave.

I too am susceptible to fire. I am killing
time until the Lord steals in like a thief.
They said They would. The day is coming—
our poor covenant snapped in half,
and I am not yet ready to reckon: second
death, shiver spell. I'm an eschatological
lover. Christocentric creature. Ascetic
aphrodisiac. If ever I needed you, it's now.

Heretic in Hermès

Desperately, I crave an appellation—
affix me *The Astonishing*, slick sobriquet,
let me levitate. Hereby swear to renounce
my silk, my martinis, the comforts
of this life cast at my feet.

Would that my mourning be whirled
into dancing—spun sugar, liquid
lumbar, knock-kneed, sick saint.

Whatsoever telegrams may come,
I am ready.

Me, my grief, its gristle. Give me
a reason for belief.

When I die, refute the historicity
of hysteria— let not my life be
chalked up to a mind immune
to miracle. Knock and the casket
top shall open— a deceit of lapwings
coughed out in my stead.

Ave Maria

In the eleventh hour, all there is left to do
is prop on one's thighs and sit a spell
with Saint Frank O'Hara. Two by two
by two— deluge, drug, die-cut dresses
oh mothers! that unforgivable surf
frothing away your youth into the vermilion
mouth of the sky— stuff of gleams,
up in flames, lest I stray, lead me kindly
all the way. It is no secret that I want to die
choking on glorious alfajores, if I must die.
No ode knows my sorrow. And in the good
morrow, did til I loved, the little chamber
in my chest an everywhere. All there is left
is my own teenage tenderness at the movies—
into the velvet limbs, fixed on the all-seeing
eye, cracked upon the skull by an unforeseen
tristesse, permitting myself to enter.

Eleven Addresses to the Lord

I.

Lord, this languish is dedicated to the project of my salivation—
long hungry, long been weary, so long the chimeras visit me
in sleep—I spin Blessed Assurance from my lips hoping for alchemy,
knowing nothing is sure, knowing there is not enough blessèd oil
in the world to make me gold. Even as I hope you are waiting to call
me, even as I know a railroad is one sort of room, even as I have tried
and failed to make a home in your heel—I've no friend like you lord,
only your feet to cleanse that I should make a home in you— I
will never touch that hem—sheared edge underturned— this flesh
never anointed enough to summon the sun—lord: I am gall—
headsick hymned to death—at every cock's crow O come—keep
me in thy bosom, even as I know a line is one sort of broken
talus, that this valediction is another sort of room— that I
could make a home in it—amen. Amen.

II.

I've been biding my rhyme— tarrying at the threshold
of the Upper Room, dying in wait. If I am to kneel three
times a day, grant me grace when it slips my bind. O god:
so many times I have begged thy pardon, pined for remission,
unable to calculate the expanse of my sin! All the weeping
widows wavering. That is, dress this chamber. The psalmist
renders you laughing. So and so begets so on. I must admit
my vanity, though rarely am I in the mood for repentance.
O bitter wine. O scorned cheek. O but I can kneel, I can beg,
I can hasten. The psalmist renders you a being with fingers,
eyelids. Such are the limitations of our minds. That our Hell
is but a preschooler's finger-painting. Sometimes I am so gindrunk
I cannot stand. I speak with my mouthful at the table— sever
my tongue O lord. Hush me. Reveal to me thy faceless face.
Lend me your earless ear. That our Heaven is but Tomorrowland.
David knew not that you have no nose. And yet you maketh
mine own. O lord, let the meditations of my heart. The words
of this filthy psalm. I cannot conceive of your creation, but I see
your work in maypop vine, in the catches of belovèd elbows,
even in the unyielding mandible of that feline which consumes
me whole.

III.

I am grateful to be placed in the hospital
for my labor. They prescribed me pyrotechnics
to soothe the ache. In the euphoria of the blaze,
there is no besuited angel, so I must still
be alive. Holy grammar of Betweenworld.
I'd been toiling. I considered
the heavy-bodied gesture of a pilgrimage
to the Styx, but I had no coin to pass.

Place one on my tongue, will you?
Do not let rigor mortis dismay.
There is a benevolence in being fed.

I have learned I ought not bargain for breath.
Holy absence of wristwatch. In your time, lord.
If it be your will.

IV.

In the little hours, I find myself coaxing apart
the strands of my nightgown, rapt with rapture.
Many times, in the little hours, under the cracked
egg of the sun, I named myself Mystic. Many
times— pills lost to the phantasmagoria
of my handbag, I wait for mania to find me,
and I incline my heart toward you.

V.

My arrival at quarter-century comes
as a shock. Here is the Good News:
Here am I, send me. Haunt, horror,
haint blue— embark with me. Collide
the champagne bottle against the hull
of my future. Hitch me hulking. Cleave
me to/from you— through marrow, through
cell— once you might have said the veil
is so thin we are one once, you might have
said go forth and tell. I am bored of been
made in your image. Bored of bearing witness
to your works. Bored of near-death devil:
I drowned and redawned and gave my life
to you, and every year the spit-sour sea
comes beckoning. Perhaps I am asking—
Give me utterance. Or, help me understand
your precious threeing. When I whine
wine winding, clutch my orphaned chin—
O darling, my little child, come in.

VI.

Doxology

Here is what I can see: A chorus of jaundiced lemons gathered in the curve of an arm, spring snow freezing the grass, a dead tabby in the street, each variegated limb shocked straight. Here is what I can tell you: Days perplex into the next and the next. Savior, every sunchoke leans its limb to you.

VII.

I seek you in the kitchen, in the garden, among the languid
olive leaves, at my footboard. I seek you in the shoebox—
beseeching for divine sight to the silent priest. But what
is the little collared man, but the little collared man? Mediation,
meditation, intercession—

I want to relish in reliquary: assembly of sacred tarsals
on display, the skull of Mary Magdalene preserved
in a space helmet.

Make me poet-prophet, I weep.
Said Augustine, doctor of grace, not yet.

VIII.

Catechism

Q: What is the chief end of human life?

A: Feet anointed with spikenard, kneeling woman drying Jesus' heels with her hair— melons, cucumbers. Leeks, garlic. Radishes livid and caked in soil, mangoes with vermilion skin, onions spiraling into their centers, children catching locusts in their teeth, wild honey, sacred scent, yoked goats and their milk: these ecstatic makings. Fashion me an artifact of new creation, visit me in my becoming— I am but a gerund racing toward you— ankles thorned by milk thistle, a damson in distress.

IX.

The word for *window* remains unsayable to me, can only be written.
The words for floodgate, chimney, channel. I won't tangle in ontology.
I am asking overflowing open. I give so little in this divine economy,
in this lopsided exchange. And yet you wake me and wake and wake.

Your many names are my anchor. A disembodied hand delivers the host.
The blood the body the blood. In my mouth you transfigure. In my vivarium.
Once, you blew life into dust. Father, (may I call you father?) thy kingdom
thy will be. On earth as it is in. Forever and ever and

X.

Petition

Penitentiary, breaking seal of sacrament,
newly minted morning. Let not revelation
lift veil, lilt liar, monastic millinery, mad mad
habit. Sans seraphim, chalk-faced cherub,
antecerebellum, doubt devour.

XI.

I know now, barefoot and smocked and cheek unturned,
that my unworthiness is by design. I do what I can to keep
steady: Worship walls bare as sucked bone. I am making
a way in the wilderness and streams in the wasteland—
every passing second untilled. For what it's worth, I brought
a little something to the altar. I have the knowledge that I
will never be redeemed. I do not expect to withstand any deluge.
No longer can I ask that you keep me ensconced in your breast.
Nor will I wait for any jasper, any agate, any emerald.
I will not wait.

Kef 21

after Henry Dumas

First there was the cash in my mouth. I was the prized pig: ponytail stretching my friendly face into a shock. There were the tributaries my piss made in the chalky dirt. Their urgency. Uttering homophones under a limestone sky. The parishioner who painted over the 20th century Jesus had it right. I am not wishing to be rendered into eternity. Nor am I wishing to be made whole.

Only I am reaching toward the sublime in me.

Open the Door

for LW, and Betty Carter

Glory be to god for a cedar waxwing poised amidst a spray of elderberries. Glory— the feeling for a love's anklet in the dark. When I sleep on my back, my palate softens and falls into my throat, and the night terrors blast through the door. Wine bolsters me enough to venture into my apprehension, trembles me toward a clearing that looks like it may ignite any second. What can fire clear in me? I used to be capable of picking locks, now my reliance on keys is limiting. Now I must ask— open the door, dear. I must get in your heart. Plenty love. Plenty plenty love. A little florida water between my breasts bolsters me enough to leave the apartment, to dedicate this verse, (albeit to letters) stilettos slicing through dusk, congregations of mosquitoes flitting overhead.

Tinnitus

On the day of your rising, I forage
through the synoptics— same
psychotic, same eye. I am waiting
for that inexorable exorcism
to quell all my worry. I feel closest
to you while transfixed on the furrow
between a belovèd's brows.
Closest where the light lives,
refracting Rococo.

On the day of my rising, I forge
a few strokes in a past hand.
Exostosis, exegesis. I have
a tendency toward adornment,
tend to get drunk on the theremin
in my head.

I won't keep you long. I only wish
to plait your hair, if you let me.
In the crimson print, your voice
parts my static. I am waking—
undressing my mirrors
of their brocade, breaking
my fast in a fury of saffron
sun—shriving, synchronous
orbit, sin-tinged singing.

Self-Portrait as Mary Magdalene in Ecstasy in the Style of Gentileschi

I retired the Mary Magdalene around my neck
to a quaint embroidered box. The pressure of her
devotion was too much to carry. I have trouble
leveling and require a soft reminder of the double
pole inside me. Seeking a refuge for my soul, where
do I go but to the State Street preacher, who proclaims
the word into a rattling portable microphone, flanked
by Macy's mothers shoving along their futuristic strollers.
My phone is dead, so I ask if by chance he has the time,
to which he replies now. Jesus is coming, been came,
come back! Supposedly, the Son knows me by name.
Supposedly if I call, he'll answer. In the morning,
having pressed on through the acute trouble,
I acknowledge how far my mind has come
from turning against and against itself. It's too hot
for anything but gazpacho. Trouble don't last.
Not always.

Bob Kaufman

I should be spent of gerunds, but I am visiting
with the "Black Rimbaud." Keeping him breathing
by way of grammar—ever-present present.
Tasked with keeping watch, I am furling
into slumber. *Could you not tarry for one hour?*
Kaufman is asking, leaning into my hatchback
in stalled traffic. These visitations come frequent,
swift; there is no simile to adequately account
for ghosts, for passing the hours with the passed
on, the beatified, the bereft, the Beat. There is
a guitar in my head too—whining and wave-licked
riffs, stadio ratic. Bob breaks years of silence with a lyric
of ships that sail forever. Bob and I are everywhere,
hold infinity as we hold fast to the last dregs of life:
Bluegreen Negroes whose deaths mean we're never dying.

Kef in D Minor

after Henry Dumas

It's a rigormortis
two-step sway.
It's the moon
which transfigures
me beyond
recognition—
crater-pull.
Even the water
within me.
I zombie
and the music
don't stop.
The lines
of my love.
My mouth
full of substance
godtongued
serpent ancient
aqueducts
of spit
and sweat.
It's a death
dance dou
dou. I don't
mean harm,
only to offer
my tenderhead
by the crown.

Celtic Cross

I thought it was a game of strategy.
Instead it was the neck of a bee-eater,
or the earthless ashes of Maria Callas:
coloratura contessa, flying into the faces
of those who loved her. Jackie Callas:
"We were helplessly eating my sister."

Instead, I flip a coin or my cards:
level palms grasping at the future
with greed. It's all chance—aleatoric
music bellowing about. Mediator
for vibration, struck tuning fork
resounding.

Grace

The nearing heat calls me in the manner I always imagined some celestial creature would, soon seeing sequins behind my eyes, seeking sequence in spliced sound: lawnmower cut with Esther Phillips' contralto whirling from the machine I've come to trust. It always gives me my sermons, always lines me up for cod liver oil like someone with my sake at heart, with stakes in my game. *"And I love him"* and I say it too much. Scrapped my altar in the second draft. Scrapped with the version of myself that sleeps vigilant at the edge of the bed. Black eye blooming. It's contact I fear. It's yielding to my call— touch, answer. Tucked in the eaves of the churchhouse, I still get the message. Still get it separated by the thin veil of the television, tarrying in the cybersanctuary. Fondue fountain free. Horoscopic heliotrope. Hagiographic haunt. I'm always keeling toward sun. No matter the ache, or the acreage. Stranded or held like grains of paradise in a palm.

Against Resistance

I walk to buy a pack of playing cards. Solitaire must be enough to quell those roaring feelings even metaphor cannot reach. Calla lily turning black from too much tending and it must be enough. Keeping the livewire at bay, keeping watch. Cigarettes in the bath stink up the studio. Desire, or the animated still image of one's own devising, minutiae of verisimilitude hanging onto its corners by a silkworm's life's work. I wrote quite a few poems before I died. Saw the same person pass across my vision as the hours turned over on their slick sides: on the sidewalk, on the street, on the perimeter of the lake, with flooded hems and the measured pace of someone harboring secrets. Water acrobatic with the heft of dailiness. I too acrobat under the weight. I isotonic exercise. Cling too cleanly, but still so much junk. Badly indebted to death, that unnameable color creeping over the ridge at daybreak. I am asking to run back the rules once more. Need to hear it, need to powder my nose, need to forsake my monogamous commitment to vegetables, delicate infidelity—a spinning top stopping somewhere.

Love Ballad

My little lapsed fanatic— when I kiss you,
a pitaya in another city leaps from a grocery
tote into the grass, into evening perspiration,
into color. I can give you so much blue.
I've grown accustomed to your iconoclastic
clavicles, must admit this missive is a declaration,
tribute to our alchemical courtship.
Golden Arches, metallic metonymy—
it's a delicate disco, bifocal to bifocal,
tripping the light fantastic in the laundromat—
throes of samedi, nearly syncope, heat
of dissociation, molecular devotion, besotted,
bewitched, bevvied, beloving.

Sketches

A radish wrenched from the dirt
My husband gently blowing a drowned
bee back to life

The days when I starved my body
have passed, but in the witching
hour, I can't stop filling myself.
Then, the looming morning: playing
Charlie Parker's "Ornithology."
Nicknamed "Bird," I consider
what it means to craft a study
of one's own species.

Trusted teacher says: in poems,
don't tell the "you" what it already knows.

I cannot tell what we know.
Only a blistered burn on my right hand,
my pleather creepers sticking
to the dive bar floor as I weep into a lager
under the slot machine glow.

Luck is limber, always bending away
but hope runs riot like a weed

Leave Don't Go Away Live

Whether by the adumbral
gardens adjacent the museum,
or as a figure in the top floor
window of my office building:
This is a tune about ardor,
though like any obedient poetic
subject, I try best to rebuke
the announcement of meaning.
But devotion likes to make
itself plain: pricked victim'd finger
blooming. They're coming to put
my landline in at week's end. They're
coming for me, can't come up for air.
There is more August yet. More
unbidden velocities. Swear I'll do right
by my heart rate, whatsoever
the pharmaceutical visions.
There is no decadent decoding.
No modular mobility. How mutable
my embouchure. Chips fall at risk,
at random. The only logic is in Threadgill's
wind.

Whoso list to hunt

I cling to the poems I committed to memory,
even through the medicines. When I reenter
the world, I am standing in my memoir,
though I'm not quite sure when. Just ticking
off the minutes until my mausoleum rings me
up. I've always craved to be hailed, held.
And stability is like grasping for a meteor
as it zips past my eyes. It's dark out there,
dark in me. I'm decked in splendor and the patent
leather I donned when I was committed

to some trickling elixir beneath my tongue—
scorched birth, syllabic lullaby, scant
lightning, sweet sleep. The devil meets me
in mirrors, and I twist my painted maw into
a smirk. I could tidy me, if I tried. I could train
my flesh into transfixion. I could recite *noli me tangere*
to my reflection, and yet I could never let me go.

Sketches (II)

The armchair whining under my new weight.
Arugula entwining around my fingers as I chop.
Dialing you up. A lithograph of you in profile,
rendered in oxblood ink.

Tapered candles drowning in their own wax.
A time-lapse of our bodies kerning toward
and away from each other in sleep. Fidelity.
A lapse.

Wounded, I veer down the gravel to the farmstand
in search of sweet corn.

I tend to trust the breaches of my mind—
those tidal, routined forgettings— ever they may
recede but they always return to me.
I trust what returns, even if it is space and not
memory. Space, at once so vast and particular,
I trust in you.

Hallucinating Reginald Shepherd on His Birthday

Your surname guides with a patient hand
as your flock lags behind. There is something
to be said about patience: about lyric that
attunes to nature, in that being human
is no more than being lapsed animal. Our
continuum has no container. Biding,
it is still possible to be kept alive via verse,
vis-à-vis alliterative light, or by field recordings
of house finches catalogued—diligent.
You look directly at the camera, as if startled
by the flash—wide-eyed and rendered
in monochrome. You, tender of pasture
and fabulist vibrations, herding sheep
and stretching your arms to span the galaxy.

Monody

I refuse to go. No shoe can hold me close
enough. No cavernous craniotomy can let
in enough light. When I leave through
the back door and the music kicks off
in my mind— full of lobster bisque
and holding on to the last fumes of warmth
before evening, I will be ready enough
to call on my dead. But for now, I will loiter
here: my thumb jumping and landing
on the island in the center of your kitchen
to the beat of "Poinciana." There isn't much
you can do but feed me. There isn't much I can
do but eat. It's as quotidian as the moment
of dissociation before your number is called
out at the deli. I refuse to go and yet I am swiftly
standing before the case.

Sketches (III)

We have moved beyond the apocalypse.
Even the docile knocks at our doors
to let us know now is the time,
have ceased. The witnesses have left

us to our fractal fornication. Our bodies are
an atomic, intimate eschaton. And my husband
is a temptress, cloying coquette. A toxic, flowering
nightshade baring its center, then receding.

I've always felt untethered, bitten my nails
to bleeding. Rapid shots: my index trailing
along their jaw, leaving amaranth in its wake.
Suspiria, daydating oneself, fish and chips
and pale ale across the street from the theater.
A sea of blurred tote bags among the rubble.

Aubade (Dysphoria)

At long last the oyster moves
between sexes as it ages, seamless
slimy shimmer shifting forth
and back. Back to the beginning:
dipping into happy hour, cocking
my hat down over my gaze,
deftly shooting back a dozen
in a half-time dance. Loosen
the saline body, blueberry
mignonette, lemon, neck-crane,
again.

What's tempting, what's teeming
what's timid, what tensile touch,
what mathematics which code me:
twinned and twined together.
Darting around a blissy Saturday.
Madwoman, maybe mollusk,
making money, making
soup season, scrubbing
the sand from leek limbs.

Obey, abide. Assume the animal
body as it slides down the hatch.
Anticipate the expanse of longing
to fill your chest chambers
when he descends the stairs
two at a time. Touch can enter
the interstices invisible to the eye
undressed. I'm a bad woman.
But Duchamp's geometry,
his second nude's staggered motion.
That's my love, his blur.
Were I better, touch could enter.

At last, I move between genders
as I age. Shifts sloppy stitching
body back back. Hypostatic union.
Hippocratic heart.

Wisdom Teeth

Churches are out of the question. I animate shadows
with my acrylic nails at dusk, a coy color pulling
across the ceiling. I was bobbing just under the surface
of anesthesia. Tigers jumped from the mouths of lilies—
I was the gossamer id at the center of a Remedios Varo.
Come closer. We have seeds to bury. We have teeth
to rend from their roots, people to submerge in the river!
Give me your hand that I may trace the lifeline. Give me
person to person. Give me hagiography. Come close.
The night-mare races ribbons across the track.
Bet your last.

Sketches (IV)

There is a haze outside the Russian Tea Room,
dampening my hair. My phone warns me that Céline
Dion's cri de cœur is too loud for my ears, but no matter.

Back home, looping the ballad, upsetting
that hair, chopping it with blunt kitchen scissors
into a shape vaguely resembling a bob.

Something in me bleats like a yearling—
anguished and new. I file a portrait
of my husband inside the band of my cigarette
case. Yearling or yearning, whichever.

I deprived my body for too long and tied
my silk kerchief too tight. I had to quench
my insatiable lunge toward scones
with cream and jam, oolong and salmon
roe, champagne.

Fuzzy, and yet.

It's all coming back to me now.

Antediluvian

Before, inside was a condition. Pardon me, conditional—before I purchased an armful of objects which would soon become a vanitas on my counter: parched lilies arching their backs like "Appalachian Spring," delicate pyramid of Black Missions rotting to death: one beheaded and seeping carnage onto the marble. This is how I tell time. Overripe. Half-past soon. Before, I was agoraphobic: contemplating whether or not to keep my standing appointment with the hypnotist. I thought she could dig me out of it. I see her veined hand in my sleep, helixing. Pardon me—I've been staring through the window: watching the wind fret the grass, watching the wind. I feel guilty. I take pre-packaged communion in front of the television. I meant ecophobic. I lied, I don't sleep. I neglected to keep my standing. I let the sun blur me into chromatic aberration—fig guts, Delft blue. I meant physicist. I meant inside is atemporal. I meant, before, inside was a persimmon, permission. I thought she could fig me out. I thought she could discover me. Forgive me.

Meaning

of the darkest color possible, that of soot, coal, the sky on a moonless night in open country, or a small hole in a hollow object, designating this color; (also) so near this as to have no recognizable color. jet-, pitch-, raven-, of coffee served without milk or cream. I enclosed in a glass some great black-bodied spiders with short legs. black plumed hawk. Fade to or from, carbon in its purest form, root, rot, celestial body incapable of emitting light, invisible to the eye: those radiations of unknown origin which pass this way through opaque bodies. tellurium, tobacco, Malevich's Square *and Goya's* Saturn Devouring His Son. *ankle, music, wing-edge, stone in the corner of the Kaaba, of deep water, of clouds, melancholia, the Duke*

of Burgundy's sleeve,
just beyond violet, lung,
magic, opal, pepper,
petroleum, hair, silk,
blue-black: as soil, as
soap, as the pupil of an
eye, as necrosis,
gunpowder . . . also with
the capital initial.

Catharsis

For the director of music. With stringed instruments.

I spend all my time mything what I had.
Every day is Sabbath— keep holy, keep
hungry, heavy head. When I say recovering,
I mean suddenly, I can regard the curvature
of cochlea, cognates and their kin. Cow's
milk is ceremony, conjure. I am sorry for
our loss, can only offer this liturgical dirge.
With stringed instruments, or accompanied
by the synth in "Seems So Long"
With a wanting hand, or the vibraphone
in "Springtime Again"

It's spring. It's spring. It's spring.

Benediction

Unable to reach me, my friends have begun sending
dried tubers in the mail. Friends, send for each other.
The time is now and now I pry open the glass to let
in the yellow. Thus I was—in the day the doubt
consumed me, and the moths by night—fellow
shipping in eclipses by lamplight. When we are
absent from one another, may the lord watch
between thee and me and thee. May there be
a beacon betwixt us. Bless, keep. Amen.

NOTES

In “Heretic in Hermes” the line, “Would that my mourning be whirled into dancing.” is a reference to Psalm 30:11.

In “Ave Maria” the lines “and in the good morrow / did til I loved, the little chamber / in my chest an everywhere” are a riff on John Donne’s poem “The Good-Morrow.”

The title “Eleven Addresses to the Lord” comes from John Berryman’s poem of the same name.

The line “I am gall” from “Eleven Addresses to the Lord” part I, comes from Gerard Manley Hopkins’s poem “I wake and feel the fell of dark, not day.”

The line “way in the wilderness and streams in the wasteland” in “Eleven Addresses to the Lord” part XI comes from Isaiah 43:19.

The term "Black Rimbaud" in the poem "Bob Kaufman" is a moniker reportedly given to poet Bob Kaufman during his time in France.

The phrase "Could you not tarry for one hour?" in "Bob Kaufman" is from Matthew 26:40.

This poem also refers to Bob Kaufman's decade-long vow of silence, which he broke by reciting his poem "All Those Ships That Never Sailed" in 1973.

The line "We were helplessly eating my sister" in "Celtic Cross" comes from Jackie Callas's book *Sisters*, in which she describes Maria Callas's ashes flying into the faces of funeral attendees as they were scattered.

The title "Love Ballad" is inspired by the song of the same name by LTD.

The title "Leave Don't Go Away Live" comes from a live performance of the song "Leave Don't Go Away" at the Chicago Jazz Festival by Jack Dejohnette, Muhal Richard Abrams, Larry Gray, Roscoe Mitchell, and Henry Threadgill in 2013.

The phrase "noli me tangere" in "Whoso list to hunt" comes from Sir Thomas Wyatt's poem "Whoso list to hunt, I know where is an hind"

The third stanza of "Aubade (Dysphoria)" makes reference to Michel Duchamp's painting *Nude Descending a Staircase No. 2*.

"Benediction" makes reference to the Mizpah prayer, found in Genesis 31:49.

ACKNOWLEDGMENTS

Many thanks to the editors of the following publications, where earlier versions of some of these poems appeared:

Ballast Journal: "Grace"; *Bat City Review*: "Theoria" and "Love Ballad"; *Bennington Review*: "Eleven Addresses to the Lord (excerpt)" and "Antediluvian"; *Berfrois*: "Commodity Fetish" and "Still Life"; *The Best American Poetry 2023*: "Antediluvian"; *The Iowa Review*: "Meaning"; *LETTERS Journal*: "St. John the Baptist Bearing Witness"; *Puerto del Sol*: "Outside" and "Discharge"; *Phoebe Journal*: "Two Wings to Veil My Face"; *Pushcart Prize Best of the Small Presses Anthology 2024*: "Self-Portrait as Mary Magdalene in Ecstasy in the Style of Gentileschi"; *Torch Literary Arts*: "Self-Portrait as Mary Magdalene in Ecstasy in the Style of Gentileschi"

I would like to express immense gratitude to the team at Pitt, including Nancy Krygowski and Jeffrey McDaniel, Alex Wolfe, Melissa Dias-Mandoly, and Lesley Rains. To my teachers, Michael Dumanis and Phillip B. Williams, for your invaluable mentorship and guidance over the years. Thank you to Derrick Austin for your incredibly generous words. To Na Chainkua Reindorf for lending your singular visual work, and to my artistic peers I. S. Jones, Marsae Lynette, and MaKshya Tolbert for your encouragement and friendship. To Christopher, my dear comrade. To my long-time beloveds; "Benediction" is yours: Jeanelle, Ashby, Ona, and Katie. And to Loïe, ever my muse. Thank you.